Anonymous

The Wyandotte fowl

Its general characteristics and advice on rearing, mating and breeding with

a chapter on judging of exhibition birds

Anonymous

The Wyandotte fowl
Its general characteristics and advice on rearing, mating and breeding with a chapter on judging of exhibition birds

ISBN/EAN: 9783337147099

Printed in Europe, USA, Canada, Australia, Japan

Cover: Foto ©Lupo / pixelio.de

More available books at **www.hansebooks.com**

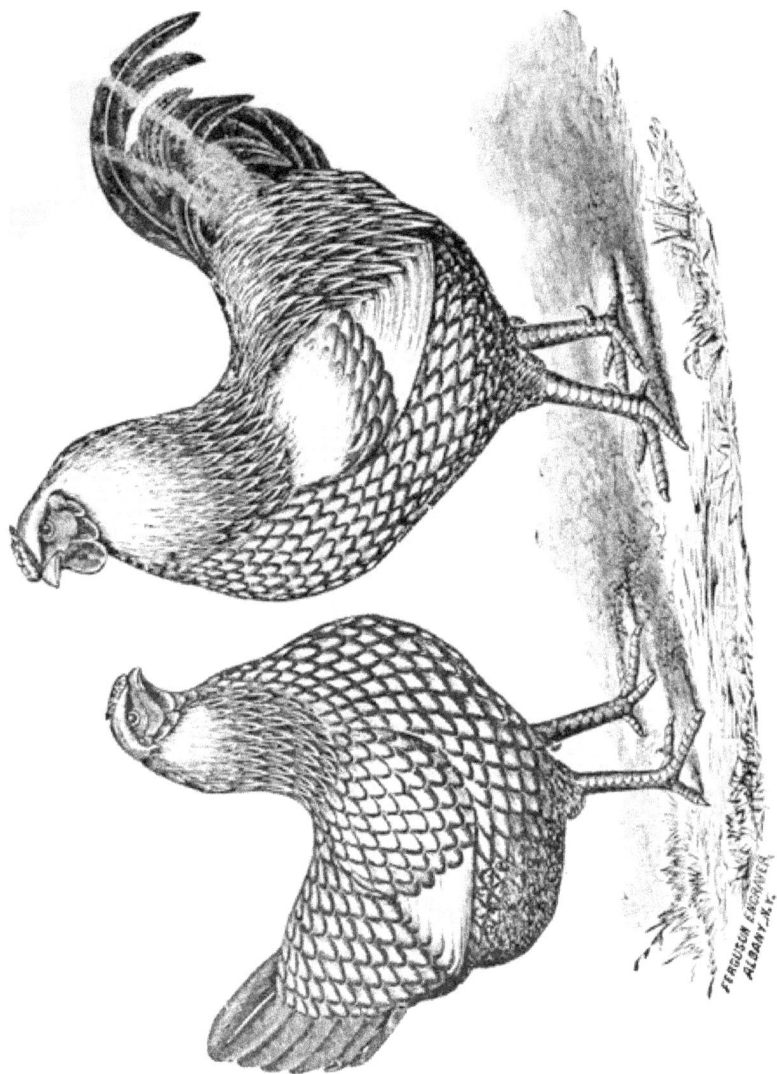

FERGUSON ENGRAVER
ALBANY N.Y.

THE

WYANDOTTE FOWL:

ITS

GENERAL CHARACTERISTICS,

AND

Advice on Rearing, Mating and Breeding,

WITH A CHAPTER ON

JUDGING OF EXHIBITION BIRDS.

BY THE

EDITORS OF THE "POULTRY MONTHLY."

WITH ILLUSTRATIONS.

ALBANY, N. Y.:
FERRIS PUBLISHING COMPANY,
Publishers of the "Poultry Monthly" and Rural Books.
1884.

BURDICK & TAYLOR,
PRINTERS,
481 BROADWAY, ALBANY, N. Y.

INTRODUCTION.

In presenting this volume to the public, we beg the indulgence of the reader to any fault or shortcoming that may appear. The belief that much experience in imparting knowledge to those of lesser experience would enable us to prepare a monograph on the Wyandotte fowl, was the moving spring which at first produced this work, and which now presents it to the poultry breeders of America in its present form.

The rage and fashion for bookmaking now-a-days is not confined to the editorial profession particularly, though it is true they have absorbed the lion's share of the work—presuming they have facts and facilities for acquiring a thorough knowledge of their subjects to entitle them to some consideration from poultrymen, especially those for whose benefit the works are designed.

We offer no apology for writing up the Wyandotte fowl We believe the time has come when the rapidly-increasing popularity of the breed demands a special place in our poultry literature. Time alone, however, may witness the rise and fall of many a promising breed; but until then the Wyandotte—America's best production—will hold its place in the foremost rank; first in utility and first in attractive plumage.

This book is designed to aid the Wyandotte breeder in the mating, breeding, feeding, management and care of his fowls. It is also designed as a hand-book for the amateur fancier and exhibitor, as well as the large class of poultrymen who are making a specialty of the breed.

We know there is room for improvement in the Wyandotte fowl; years of skillful breeding will bring about a great change for the better; we are looking hopefully to the near future to attain that promising result; soon we shall have a fowl as perfect in reproduction as any of the old breeds; and as an aid to the good work we offer this volume.

EDITORS POULTRY MONTHLY.

WYANDOTTES.

BEYOND the newspaper articles, which are short and of general import, there has sprung up a demand for something more exhaustive regarding the mode of breeding and of judging, with the history of the origin of the breed. This can best be furnished in book form, which leads us in this treatise to give to our patrons a work complete in itself; a hand-book of the breed which shall enable the novice to rear, mate, breed and judge the race of fowls herein named. First we consider

ITS ORIGIN.

This breed, not new, but recently admitted to the American Standard, has been the result of the following breeding and circumstances, having had many names and suggestions of names:

It was, without doubt, the intention with the first cross to produce an improved Cochin Bantam, the cross being a Sebright Bantam cock with a Cochin hen. When the size proved too large they were offered and illustrated as Sebright Cochins. This suggested the cross of Silver Spangled Hamburgs with Buff Cochins. These two crosses mingled with another cross with a half-Buder and Cochin hen, became the blood mixture of the early birds offered to the American Poultry Association as American Sebrights. Their friends could not agree as to the comb being single or double, as it was then expressed, and the name being so suggestive of an American Bantam, the request was refused and the matter referred back to a committee.

About the same time, a cross of a Silver Hamburg with a Dark Brahma hen produced a still more desirable type, having pea combs. Mr. Kidder, of Northampton, contended earnestly for this characteristic being accepted as the regulation. But these crosses, while being bred by themselves, presented troublesome features of both feathered and smooth legs, single and rose, also pea and rose combs. The best birds were called Eurekas. When these two wings, or original crosses, were brought together, more uniform specimens were produced, the Hamburg blood being in the greater proportion, the combs, in the majority of cases, assumed a more rose appearance, though smaller and closer to the head, the feathers disappeared from the legs, yet the golden color of skin and legs remained. The males, in color, reverted strongly to Dark Brahma color, and the females gave evidence of their Hamburg ancestry by presenting a laced plumage.

It was our lot to publish a standard for them under the name of Hambletonians. This brought the breed into earnest discussion, and gave it a new interest, the name being discussed, and other names suggested, among which were Columbias, Ambrights, Americans, in addition to those already mentioned.

Thus has the race been before the people for twelve years or more, and for six years has had the attention of poultry fanciers brought in a special manner to its merits. It was better perfected when accepted by the American Poultry Association than was the Plymouth Rock at the time of its adoption, for it was six years after it was reported back to its committee before its final adoption and admittance into the "Standard of Excellence" as Wyandottes.

The struggle has been hard. Its breeders deserve credit for their fidelity to the race, and the breed is truly one of practical merit; for as broilers it has no equal, and for small size roasters it is excellent, while its laying qualities are first-class.

CHARACTERISTICS.

The cock should approach the Brahma shape of body, and have short neck, short legs, with a close, low and rose comb —not a fully developed Hamburg comb—the bars of the wing distinctively developed in a double or spangled bar, so to speak, being a combination of the Dark Brahma and Hamburg characteristics in this point of the wings, of which we shall speak more fully in our chapter on judging.

The female should be long in body, the cushion slightly raised to a convex sweep from hackle to saddle, moderately short in neck and legs, the latter being golden yellow in color.

The fowls grow more rapidly than the Plymouth Rocks, are shorter bodied and more compact. Yet this is against the breed in its merit as an egg-producer, as compared to what it might be if a little longer in the body. We recommend that it should be bred for more length of body. In recent experiments in other breeds, it is shown that the longer the body and closer the feathering, the larger and more numerous the eggs.

The race, however, is hardy, and its fecundity remarkable. With care in the selection of color of plumage, care to breed from such females as lay large, dark-colored eggs, and from males that are the sons of hens long in body and layers of large cinnamon-colored eggs, the race can be carried to a high degree of merit, that few, if any, other breeds can excel.

This is pre-eminently the farmer's and poulterer's breed of America, and will in a large measure supplant many of the medium-sized breeds in and for American use. The demand for golden-hued poultry will place the breed in advance of the Dorking and French varieties, while its fine grain and tender, juicy condition and nice flavor will supplant the Plymouth Rock and Dominique.

This autocrat of American origin must stand at the head of all medium and small-sized poultry stock for practical poultry culture; while, as an exhibition specimen, it is fast finding friends. During its first season as such, and it first season as an American Poultry Association variety, it has commanded fifty dollars a pair at Worcester, while fifty dollars was paid for a pair of pullets from a disqualified pen at the New York exhibition; prices ranging from twenty-five dollars to seventy-five dollars a pair are being made now on the eve of its second exhibition season, which bids fair to carry the race to as high figures as any one of its predecessors have reached. Certain it is, that its merits find a rival only in the Light Brahma, and that breed being an Asiatic, does not come in competition as show or poultry stock; the respective points of merit being in a different direction, yet strongly related, making these two breeds to be associated in each and every poultry yard where both practical and show merits are to be obtained. The Wyandotte breed for broilers " fills the bill," so to speak; they grow three weeks quicker than Plymouth Rocks, and fully one month quicker to roasting excellence than the Light Brahmas; therefore, for the wants of summer and fall demands of the poultry market, one makes a sad mistake when he substitutes any other breed. The consumption of fifteen thousand broilers per day at Coney Island alone, a proportionate quantity at Long Branch, Nantasket, Bar Harbor, White Mountains and other summer resorts, with a large and constant city trade, is building up each and every day this already monstrous poultry and egg demand of our land, until not less than six hundred millions of dollars must now be considered the yearly product, of which far more than its average amount will, in coming years, be

demanded of this now considered new breed of American
fowls.

May, 1881, we published a standard for Hambletonians
(the name then selected for this breed), which was the basis
of the standard adopted by the American Poultry Association, and will give the novice a very correct idea, without our
encroaching upon the copyright of the American Poultry
Association — the publishing of which may be said to have
done more to bring the breed permanently before the poultry
breeders, and its merit into consideration, than all its friends.
This gave it nearly two years of breeding of the same
influence as now the breed feels from the standard adopted
by the American Poultry Association.   Thus the breed may
be said to have been in a far more perfect state of breeding
when it was accepted than any other new breed previous to
its adoption.   What we had to say of them as Hambletonians
will be found in the following, omitting the disqualifications,
as it may confuse, and for which we refer the reader to the
American Poultry Association Standard of Excellence:

HAMBLETONIANS.

THE COCK.

Symmetry.—The combination of all the parts in harmony,
as seen in specimens possessing a well-arched neck, full
flowing hackle, short, well-turned back, a prominent, roundly
moulded breast, body deep and round at the sides, fluff full,
tail well spread at its base; possessing a graceful, elastic
carriage.

Value of this section, ten points.

Weight.—To be determined by the scale, deducting at
the rate of two points to the pound for all deficit of perfect
standard weight, that being nine and a half pounds for cocks,
eight pounds for cockerels, eight pounds for hens, six and
a half for pullets—giving no credit for any excess of weight.

Value, ten points.

Condition.—Under this head we consider disease—scaly legs, soiled and broken plumage (the damage by soil to surface, or breaking of plumage, incident to proper cooping and confinement to show-pen, excepted).

Value, six points.

Head.—Short, skull broad, plumage of same silvery white, face bright red, eyes bay color and bright, beak yellow, with heavy stripe down the upper mandible of a dark horn color, apparently stout at base and well curved to point.

Value, six points.

Comb.—Rose, low and flat, rather wide in rear, wider at base, with less prominence of spike than the Hamburg, the top surface nicely undulated with minute points.

Value, eight points.

Ear-lobes and Wattles.—Ear-lobes well developed, long and pendulous; wattles fine in texture, quite translucent and hanging somewhat below the ear-lobes.

Neck.—Short, well arched, with very full hackle, plumage silver grey, heavily striped with black, terminating in a black point, the outer edge of the lacing near the point being frosted with black.

Value, eight points.

Back.—Broad and short, by aid of wing plumage appearing flat at the shoulders—plumage in under color slate—web of feather light straw, approaching silvery white; saddle full, broad, preserving a concave sweep from back to tail; under color dark slate or black, web light straw striped with black, giving a black point to the feather.

Value, eight points.

Breast and Body.—Very broad, medium deep and prominent; plumage of under color slate, web black with very narrow white stripe to center, the breast unruffled, appearing quite black (see fig. No. 1); body thick and round at side, giving a blocky, heavy appearance; plumage in under color slate, web black, slightly frosted with grey.

Value, ten points.

FIG. No. 1. FIG. No. 2.

Wings.—Of medium size and nicely folded to the side,
primaries black, the outer edge laced with silver grey; secondaries black on inside web, the outside web having a
black stripe next to quill and round the point, the outer
edge having a wide, very light straw colored or silver grey
lacing; wing coverts nearly white, with a black stripe through
the center that widens at point of feather, producing a
double spangled bar across the wing; wing bows nearly
black, shoulder coverts slate in under color, web of same
silvery grey.

Value, ten points.

Tail.—Well developed and well spread at base, and filled up underneath with black curling feathers; sickles of medium length, black in cockerels, may become laced with white near the base in cocks; tail coverlets black, lesser coverlets having an edging of very light straw color or white, generally following the color of saddle.

Value, seven points.

Fluff.—Full and broad behind, and covered with a downy plumage; dark slate colored, powdered with grey.

Value, five points.

Legs and Toes.—Thighs short and strong, and well covered with soft, almost webless feathers, in color black posted with grey; shanks medium long, scale yellow and free from feathers; toes straight and strong, of same color as shanks.

Value, seven points.

THE HEN.

Symmetry.—To be considered as in the male, giving a low carriage to female as compared to the cock.

Value, ten points.

Weight.—Same application as in cock.

Value, ten points.

Condition.—Application as for males.

Value, six points.

Head.—Medium long, skull broad, plumage white striped with black, face deep red, eyes bay in color, beak nearly dark horn color, running into yellow on lower edge of mandible, rather short and well curved to point.

Value, six points.

Comb.—Rose, base broad and flat upon the skull, spike not prominent as in Hamburgs, top surface thickly studded with minute points, rich red in color.

Value, eight points.

Ear-lobes and Wattles.—Ear-lobes pendulous and hanging, lower lines horizontal with wattles, which are longest from beak to ear-lobe, but quite prominent, and in color rich red.

Value, five points.

Neck.—Short, full in plumage, color black, laced with narrow white lacing to side of feather, but terminating in a black point to the same.

Value, ten points.

Back.—Short and apparently wide at shoulder, saddle or cushion full, under color dark slate or black, web of feather black with white centers. the white slightly penciled with black. (See fig. No. 2.)

Value, ten points.

Breast.—Breast more broad than deep, yet very prominent, giving promise of breast meat; plumage slate in under color, web white, laced with black, lacing heaviest at point. (See fig. No. 3.)

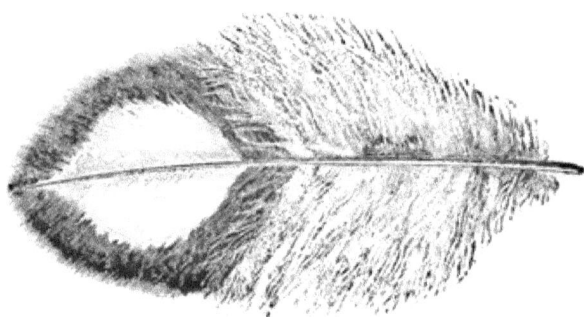

Fig. No. 3.

Body.—Short and round at sides, and medium deep; plumage slate in under color, tip of feather black, with very narrow white stripe in center, running into black, frosted with grey near the thighs. (See fig. No. 1.)

Value, ten points.

Wings.—Medium in size, and nicely folded; primaries black, with lower edge laced with white; secondaries black

on inside web, and round tip of feather of outer web, having
a narrow stripe of black next to quill of feather, with wide
white stripes on outer edge, which is penciled with black
near the end thereof; wing and shoulder coverts black or
dark slate in under color, with web laced with black, having
white centers penciled with black (see fig. 4), the black lacing growing wider as it approaches the wing bow, which is
nearly and may be quite black.

Value, ten points.

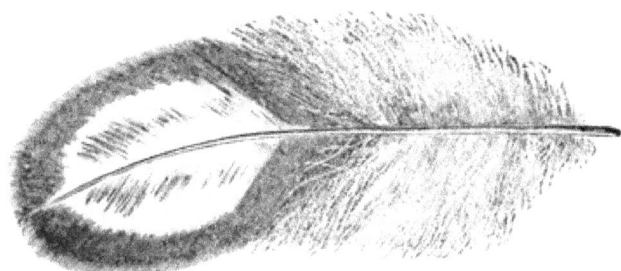

FIG. NO. 4.

Tail.—Fairly developed, wide spread at base, color black,
coverlets black, slightly penciled with white.

Value, six points.

Fluff.—Broad and full, balancing the heavy breast, giving
a wide appearance from behind, and suggesting an equal
amount of posterior and breast meat; plumage abundant,
soft and fluffy, color dark slate powdered with white.

Value, five points.

Legs and Toes.—Thighs short and well covered with black,
quite fluffy feathers, shanks rather short in comparison to
the male, color medium shade of yellow; toes medium long,
straight, strong and of same color as the shanks.

Value, seven points.

Symmetry.....................	10 points.
Weight	10 "
Condition....................	6 "
Head........	6 "
Comb........................	8 "
Ear-lobes and wattles...........	5 "
Neck........................	8 "
Back	8 "
Breast and body...............	10 "
Wings	10 "
Tail........................	7 "
Fluff.......................	5 "
Legs and toes.................	7 "
Total......................	100 points.

This proposed standard, as before stated, engendered quite a discussion, and gave the breed a new impetus in the hands of the breeders, which has carried it to the front rank of American poultry. The names suggested were Ambrights and Columbias, in addition to those already mentioned, but the discussion settled down to Wyandottes at the meeting at Worcester, 1883.

REARING.

Health and vigor certainly now exist in the breed, and can be maintained by care and feeding; the most important feature is the housing of them during the winter months.

We find in our experience that hens must have the open air each and every day to be able to lay eggs that will hatch in winter and early spring.

Such a house as the one we represent in Figure 7, page 32. could be converted into a shed and house, or both, at will. so that from ten to three o'clock each day during the winter months the flock could have the use of an open shed to take their sun and dust bath in, and in which to scratch for bits of meat and grain, which should be worked into the sandy loom to induce the exercise so much needed in both fowls and beasts. Especially is this shed necessary for healthy fowls and a large production of eggs, in the fact that fowls need seven times more air, in proportion to their weight, than does man or beast, for their heart beats one hundred and fifty times each moment, and they never perspire.

During the life of the chickens from eighteen to twenty-four weeks old, they are liable to suffer from distemper, so called, and at the same time they will be observed to be dropping their immature tails and hackles, and the adult plumage is growing very rapidly. If, during this period, you use bromide of potassium in the water, at the rate of two grains per chick, every other day for ten days, you will find it very beneficial, and as the distemper is manifest in a greater or less degree of thirst, the dose adjusts itself to the case; but if the case be a severe one, and the chicks neither eat nor drink, from the effects of a swollen head and a throat filled with canker, then gargle the throat with kerosene oil, and give three grains of bromide dissolved in milk—one-half gill—turning it into the crop, or administering the bromide in a bit of bread in pill form, sustaining the chick by a milk diet three to four days; this treatment generally effects a cure. If care at this time be taken, no real cases of roup need be had. Fowls suffering long with roup are not good ones to use as breeders.

The best feed for your chickens up to two weeks old, is a meal made of fifteen pounds of oats, twenty pounds of corn, ten pounds of barley and five pounds of wheat bran, ground together, and made into a bread as you make your corn cake for breakfast; bake hard and crumble into scalded milk; give no water until two weeks old; the milk is all the liquid required. One need not lose a chick if this be faithfully observed. After that age, scald the meal for the morning feed, and give cracked corn, oats, wheat and barley for balance of day. This manner of feeding hens will be found to produce twenty per cent. more eggs than the old way. This meal contains in its make-up, seventeen and one-half per cent. muscle, one and seven-eighths per cent. bone, sixty-eight per cent. fat, and, like milk, is a perfect food for both chicks and fowls, and by its use we obtain chicks at twelve weeks old, fully twenty per cent. larger than those fed in any other way.

Colonize the flocks or broods of chickens. One can raise in one flock one hundred chickens; that is, they may be fed and reared in one inclosure, by brooding twenty in a place at night. The best plan, where ample room makes it feasable, is to colonize them about the farm in groups, by placing a hen and twenty chicks in a coop thirty inches square, the coops being some thirty feet apart; as the chicks become weaned, they return at night, each flock to its respective coop. Five such broods can be placed in one locality to be fed together, but they must be within three weeks of the same age; then they will grow up of nice average merit. These groups of one hundred each may dot the farm all over, and all do well, while to place three or four hundred together, of different ages, will prove a failure.

As soon as the young males become salacious, divide the sex, feed the males largely of corn and barley, to fatten them in the shortest time possible, killing for broilers all that are not strictly first-class.

The females should be fed wheat, meat and vegetables in variety, the object being to produce bone and muscle growth and egg producing condition. A hen that is a prime producer of eggs, like a cow that produces largely at the pail, carries very little fat. But at show times, if you are desirous of exhibiting, to get the best possible gloss of plumage and weight, corn should be used freely,

the birds should be kept in a clean house that has a depth of
four inches of clean sandy loom, covered with cut straw, in
which they can scratch and dust—in which case one need
not resort to the wash tub, only to sponge the head, face,
comb and legs, when put in the show coop.

MATING.

The mating of this race of birds will not differ much from
that of other strains of fowls. To secure type and color, a
course of in-breeding must be followed, to produce a line
of sires for subsequent breeding, while size and large and
dark colored egg production must be the first starting point
in the females. If, when perfected, the dams of one family
are introduced to the perfectly bred sires, we will have a
race to breed from as true as our Plymouth Rocks, Brown
Leghorns, Dominiques or Hamburgs.

In language other than the standard, the sire, if a cockerel,
should weigh not less than seven and a half pounds, have
short neck, tail and legs; short shanks, yellow as gold; full
round breast, that should show nearly black, yet the feathers
of the same should have a small white center; flat of back
silver grey, neck and saddle silver grey striped with black,
wings as found in the standard, also the tail. To speak of
the wing, the bar should be dotted by diamond shaped white
spots, which give the appearance of a double spangled
bar. The comb should be a rose comb, but close
down, the base nearly as wide as the crown; the spike
smaller and conform more to the shape of the head as compared to that of a perfect Hamburg comb. The desire to
breed a perfect Hamburg comb is wrong, for to do it will,
of necessity, run the rest of the breed into more Hamburg
shape, which is too narrow for a good Wyandotte. It will
be noticed that birds of finest plumage and finest shape
incline to Brahma combs; or, in other words, those speci-

mens that come with pea combs are generally clearer in the
silver color, stripe of neck and saddle than those having
large Hamburg-shaped combs. Thus we assert the perfect
comb to be the small one indicated, by adding just enough
to the pea comb to convert it into a very low rose comb,
and such should be the comb sought for your typical sire.
In general color, let him be one that we should call dark for
the race, yet not one of the dark, smutty specimens we
often see.

To such a male mate those pullets that seem the embodi-
ment of the standard, but on examination prove too light,
the fluff shading light; also those pullets that present the
excellence described by the standard, and such will be found
the most perfect mating to secure the largest number of
points in the whole flock. While, to secure cockerels of prime
show qualities, these perfect sires with perfect wing bars,
mated to the medium light specimens in the females, will
produce a large per centage, yet you will lose quality in
the female stock.

To secure the greatest excellence in the female line,
expecting to condemn to the broiler market a very large
share of the males, we advise females dark to appearance,
yet having the white centers well defined in plumage; or,
in other words, those pullets that have wide black lacing to
plumage, and wide dark stripes in hackles, and dark slate
colored fluff, may be mated to males that are light in color,
having light narrow wing bars; but, like the Plymouth
Rock, for perfect mating, perfect standard described males
and females are necessary. Scrubs can only be used in
cases of necessity; in which cases dark males and the light
females should be the mating, and you should kill all males;
for no sire, the get of extreme color mating, as a rule, is a
good breeder of standard color, even if he possesses it
himself. We hope the experience of the Plymouth Rock
breeders may avail here, and all the breeders of Wyandottes

2

will kill all specimens under eighty-five points, for they will
the sooner reach perfection and stop the spread of impure
blood, which otherwise will stand in the way of sales of
good birds. There is no economy in the use or sale of
scrub stock for breeding purposes.

BREEDING TO A STRAIN.

In introducing a new strain to public patronage, a few
far-seeing fanciers have bred their stock to some particular
strain of blood that has found its typical representation in a
particular sire—a male whose characteristics have been, or
are to be, transmitted to future generations, to wit: one
retaining in all breeding stock a large share of his blood;
such persons assuming the position, and rightly, that fully
one-eighth of all blood is consumed in maintaining the strain
in a healthy, vigorous, feeding condition. This, we think,
can be easily proved by in-and-in breeding for four generations ; invariably in the third generation the eggs hatch
tolerably well, the fourth one nearly, and, in many cases,
entirely stale. Thus, while we figure the blood out arith-
matically, seven-eighths become pure, for the other one-
eighth is exhausted in sustaining the strain. Such fanciers,
in catering for the needs of their patrons, introduce female
blood only, breeding the first cross back to sire, the second
generation to another sire of pure blood of the desired strain,
and all males that are produced in type and color of the
original progeny are ready for their patrons, who can purchase of them, saving themselves from all this trouble, still
breeding birds of like blood as the breeder in question, he
being only one season in advance, and the purchaser thus
saved all experiments which he has had, and can well
afford to pay a fair price for such males and the protection
it gives.

For each breeder to do this, involves work and care, to be

relieved of which, when one can secure birds of a reliable worker in this line, affords great relief.

It pays best to mate to secure the greatest number of fine females; therefore, it pays nine out of every ten to buy males of the tenth, who will do this work for them. Breeders who have an eye to this trade in other breeds, generally mate a yard to this end each season, from which they do not sell eggs to anyone, for the reason that males from this particular pen become fit mates for whoever sends for male blood, while, as a rule, the females become the breeding pens for their particular strain, mated to the male of the line having the seven-eighths blood of this particular strain, whose new blood is drawn from a different source than the one offered for sale, and again secure for themselves a new lot of pure males, from which they again produce a new set of males.

To be successful, one has to look beyond the present—for future generations—and back through several generations if he would breed with that accuracy, that others, while examining birds here and there, may be able to recognize them, in form and color, to be of "his sort," as they say of Booth, Bates and other families of cattle, and like recognized types and progeny of noted sires in horses. This care and work is the excitement and interest which makes enthusiastic fanciers.

HOW TO JUDGE WYANDOTTES.

[For disqualifications see Standard of Excellence.]

We have endeavored to place at the head of our article, "How to Judge Wyandottes," a typical representative cut of the race, in all the prominent parts of general observation.

THE COCK.

Symmetry.—In considering this, we notice every defect in it, and punish the same more severely than the same defect in the female, because of the fact that it is expected that he will transmit that quality in a greater degree than does the female. Symmetry can be said to be harmony of perfect parts, and when symmetry is perfect, we certainly have no occasion to look for defects of form in sections. Then defect in color, or disease of plumage, comes into consideration. A male with long legs and long neck, bony body, in fact, long in the joints, could, however, be reasonably symmetric, yet be faulty in all these points. As a rule, defects in symmetry are sure to be accompanied with as many points of defect in other sections.

So we say, if the neck be long and not well arched, we cut a point; if the back be not flat, and is long, out of proportion, cut a point; if the tail be carried perpendicular, cut a point; if the breast be cut away, not full and round, cut a point; if fluff be scant, the bird being pinched behind the legs, one-half to a full point; if the tail be drooping, also one-half to a full point. You see that all these are failures of different sections in their shape, and not growing together in a harmonious way; thus symmetry is defective. There is no question but that a bird by the scale of points would be as well and more justly judged if this clause had never appeared in the scale of points, for all cuts in symmetry are but a second cut for a defect to be punished in after sections, and the breeder must not fail to consider this, and reckon on it in selecting his birds for exhibition. Even the comb, if large and of bad shape, will affect the cut line of symmetry from one-half to a full point.

Size.—This is affected only by the use of the scales, the specimen losing two points to the pound for all deficit in standard weight.

Condition.—This refers to the bird's health and cleanliness. Some judges, under this head, cut for broken plumage, while others consider all broken plumage in the sections in which it occurs, as the visitors at an exhibition understand such awards best. Fowls suffering with distemper and disease of head are cut from one to three points; a scurvy, or "black comb," one point; scaly legs, from one to three points; soiled, injured plumage, from one to three points; slight surface soiling, incident to cooping of the sexes and transit to exhibition, should not be cut; a judge can readily tell if the birds have had proper care, and all unavoidable soiling is allowed to go uncut.

Head.—This should be short, and crown broad, the plumage silver white; therefore, if it be narrow in the crown, or long or snaky, to use the expression, cut one point; if eyes be other color than bay, cut one point; if beak be wholly black or not well arched, cut one point for each; it should be dark horn color, shading to yellow at the point.

Comb.—If the comb be large, standing high, cut from one to two points; if "clubbed," having no spike, cut one to two points, for only when low and close fitting to head, with small spike, oval in front, can it be said to be perfect. Many of the cuts mislead the breeder into the belief that the comb should be fully developed, like the Hamburg, and of Hamburg shape, when a perfect Wyandotte comb should be nearly, if not quite, as wide at the base as crown; the spike conforming more to the skull than does the Hamburg, for a comb so large as to fall to either side disqualifies the specimen altogether.

Wattles and Ear-lobes.—A perfect colored ear-lobe and wattle should be bright red. As a rule, ear-lobes get cut only when tainted with foreign color, an encrusted surface, enamel, as it is called, like that of Spanish breeds; for if the ear be covered wholly by this white or yellow opaque substance, the bird is disqualified; but if partially tainted, it is cut from one to three points; if, in the judgment of the judge, three points will not punish the defect, he should promptly disqualify. The wattles may be wrinkled or torn by fighting, which seldom appears in condition to be cut more than one-half to one point; when both wattles are missing, we cut two points. Perfectly red, and smooth and fine in texture being the perfect condition of this section.

Neck.—Should be short and well arched. When long or carried forward, losing that nice arch desired, cut from one-half to one point. If the hackle be short and not abundant, cut a point. If the color be white, or insufficiently striped, being brown in the stripe instead of black, the specimen should then be punished from one to three points. If the neck be smutty black, the plumage losing the nice silver lacing to the feather, cut from one to three points, as in degree. If the plumage that should be silvery white be straw color or yellow, cut from one to two points, for a neck can only be called perfect that is well arched and in plumage is a silver gray striped to a point with black.

Back—Is short and flat at shoulder, at least has that appearance; the feathers from the arm of the wing making a flat surface at the juncture with hackle; in color these are silvery white. When the wings are set on low it shows the true shape of the back, which would look oval and narrow, injuring the symmetry; in this case, cut one point. If the saddle be silvery gray, having no black stripe in center of feather, cut from one to two and a half points, as it fails. If the silver color be tarnished to look straw color or bronze and yellow, cut from one to three, as in degree; these mixed colors of yellow and bronze mar its beauty. If the saddle be scant, allowing the tail to cut through, cut a point. If the saddle plumage be short, not full about the tail, cut a point.

Breast and Body.—First feel of breast bone, if crooked cut one point. If the breast fails to be broad and round cut one-half to one and a half. If the plumage be light, having a very narrow black lacing, cut one point. If the lacing be wide and brown, not black, cut one point. If the breast have solid black feathers in it, cut from one to three points; but if solid black or white, disqualify the specimen; a proper plumage is black with white centers; this meaning the border or lacing very wide and black.

The body should be thick and deep in front of thighs to be perfect. If flat at sides, cut a point; if not deep, being slender and shrunken in fluff, one point. If plumage be white, cut one point; a perfect color being slate in under color, with black web; the fluffy surface near thighs being slightly frosted with white.

Wings.—If they fail wholly in the bars, cut three points, diminishing the cut as the perfect bar is developed. The bar to be perfect should present a spangled double-bar, as the Standard expresses it. If you examine you will find the feathers of the wing coverts have a black line along the shaft, widening at the point into a spear-head or spangle. Now, the lapping of the coverts makes the bar, the lesser reaching the outer bar by the point of the feather, making an absolutely perfect specimen — a single bar with diamond white spots through the center of the bar. So essential to their beauty is this heavy bar that judges cut lightly when the wing is so heavy as to present a full solid or Dark Brahma bar, as it is called, yet it should be cut one-half to a full point, and considered as next best to what has been described as perfect. If the wing be poorly folded, cut from one to three points, the latter when the primaries fold outside the secondaries. Primaries three-quarters white should be cut one point for each wing; wholly black, the same; secondaries, wholly white, one point each wing; if wholly black, thus showing a black tip instead of white, cut from one to two points; lesser coverts wholly black, one to two points.

Tail.—If it be not well spread at base, one point. If the sickles are straight in form of a scimiter, cut one point. If the sickles be white, one to two points, as in degree. If the lesser sickles or tail coverts, as they aer called, are tarnished with white, cut one to two points, as in degree. Lesser coverts wholly white or silver colored, one point. If the tail be carried squirrel, one to two points; when carried perpendicular, one point.

Fluff.—If pinched, cut one point; if other than dark slate color, cut from one to two points, as it shall approach to white; the white frosting on a dark slate being the perfect color.

Legs and Toes.—If the thighs are long and small, cut one point; if plumage of same be white, cut one point; shanks long and slim, cut one point; if pale yellow, cut one point; cutting one point for each crooked toe. If feathers appear on the shanks, or if legs and toes be any other color than yellow—if straw color, they should be cut one and one-half points; if the front be clouded with a dusky color, the rear of the shank being yellow, cut one and one-half points; but the legs being wholly flesh color, blue, willow or black, disqualifies.

THE HEN.

Symmetry.—If the back have a concave sweep to tail, showing no fullness to cushion, cut one-half point. If so flat as to allow tail to cut through, cut a full point. If narrow in

breast, cut one point. If tail drops low or so small as to
be covered by the cushion (unless in moulting), cut one
point for each of these defects. If long in legs and neck,
cut a point.

Condition.—Same conditions apply here as described in
the male.

Head.—If snaky, having a narrow skull beyond a reason-
able feminine comparison to that of the cock, cut one point.
If depressed at base, giving a long appearance to beak, cut
one point. If comb and face be black or purple, not red,
cut one point; beak wholly dark horn color or flesh color,
cut one point. If plumage be other than silver gray, cut
one-half to one point.

Comb.—Should be small and close down on the head to
be perfect. If large, cut one point. If large and irregular
in shape, from one to two and one-half points, as in degree.
If falling to either side of head, disqualify, it being subject
to the same cuts and conditions as described for the male.

Ear-lobes and Wattles.—In the hen these are by no means
so largely developed as in the male, yet the lobes are quite
prominent and the wattles fairly developed into a well-
rounded size; the ear-lobes being less liable to the enamel
coating so objectionable; but when this coating appears, it
is to be cut from one to three points, as it approaches
having the whole surface covered, when, like the male, she
must be disqualified. We would not cut the specimen if
the wattles were ever so small, but if absolutely wanting,
as is sometimes the case, we must cut two points. If
wrinkled or afflicted with bunches, the effect of congealed
pus, the result of roup or chill, then cut from one to two
points, as seems just.

Neck.—If long and not arched, cut from one to two points,
but one-half to one point is as bad a defect of this nature as
we often find. If the stripe in the silver gray be wide at
the point, giving a blotched appearance, cut from one to

three points, as it approaches a black ring at the base of
hackle, and one-half to two points as the silver gray shall
shade to a yellow or deep straw color.

Back.—By the aid of the wing plumage the back under
the base of hackle seems flat in good specimens; the plumage being white, heavily laced with black, and seldom
suffers unless the wings are set so low down as to give an
oval, narrow look to the back at its juncture with the hackle,
in which case cut one-half to one point. The cushion,
as the saddle in females is called, has just rise enough to
give it a slight convex sweep from hackle to tail; when flat,
cut one-half point; when so flat as to part at tail, cut one to
one and a half. If the plumage be white, laced with black,
or the white centers be minutely penciled with black, they
are not to be cut, but if by the center penciling or other
cause the light part of the plumage has a bricky or bronzed
look or color, cut from one-half to two points, as in degree.
Any deformity of the back is a disqualification.

Body.—The body should be deep, which gives a short
appearance, but as long as can be and not look long in the
structure, for we recognize the use of a long body for egg
production. If the body be wedge-shaped, not round at
the sides, cut a point. If plumage be white, cut a point.
If wholly black, cut one-half point. It should be dark slate,
with small white centers, the fluffy, fraying-finish at thighs
being frosty white.

Wings.—If primaries fold badly, cut from one-half to
three points, as they approach to folding outside of secondaries. If primaries be white, cut one point for each wing,
(except the narrow outer edge, which should be white). If
the secondaries be black on outside of web, failing to round
the tip of the feather so as to give the scollop finish to the
secondaries when folded, cut from one-half to one point.
If secondaries are wholly white, cut two points; if set low
down, giving the appearance of long and round back, cut

one point.   If the white center of coverts be much penciled, cut one point; if coverts be wholly white, cut two points.

Tail.—If pinched into a pointed Cochin shape, cut one point; if the tail proper be tinged with white, cut one-half to two points.   If the coverts be black, or black with centers white and penciled somewhat, they should go uncut. If the light color in them be straw-color or bronzy, cut a point.   If the tail be carried upright, one point; if squirrel, one and one-half to two points.

Fluff.—Here is where many hens fail in color.   A prime color being a dark slate color, nicely frosted with white; when wholly white, cut one to one and one-half points; one-half for a less defect; if pinched, one point.

Legs and Toes.—If the thighs are wholly white, cut one point ; they should be black powdered with white.   If long in the thigh, cut one point.   If shanks or toes be clouded with smoky or greenish color, cut from one to two points, as in degree; black scales, one-half to two points.   If the legs be other than shaded from yellow to straw color, then disqualify.   Toes, cut one point for each crooked one; if a toe be amputated at the second joint, cut one point; and one-half point for one cut off at tip; but a broken toe-nail should not be cut.

Reader, have you birds that can stand this application of the Standard and score 92 to 93 1-2 points?   If so, you surely have exhibition birds; and if by this test they score 85 to 93 points, you can surely say your stock is first class and as good as any breeder's in the land, and to exhibit in pairs and breeding pens at the next exhibitions would be a source of profit to you in the way of an advertisement and bring your stock to the notice of the breeding public.   No matter how fine your specimens, nearly all of them may be helped up to an extra point of merit if care is taken to put them in the best possible condition in flesh, to cleanse the comb and face by washing in alcohol and water, and the

shanks in soapsuds, brushing all dirt and filth out from
under the edge of the scales. You know that pullets moult
twice before they lay. Now, if they have been raised in a
close pen, with insufficient grass and meat in their diet, they
will not moult clean the second time, and if you will pick
a pullet up and examine her you will see that while she
looked fine at a few rods' distance, she has many rusty old
feathers in her back; these should be removed six weeks
before show time, or a cut of one point she will surely suffer
at the hands of the judge. This care, with pains to furnish
a generous diet of meat, corn and a few oats for the three
weeks previous to exhibiting, will secure you success in the
show room.

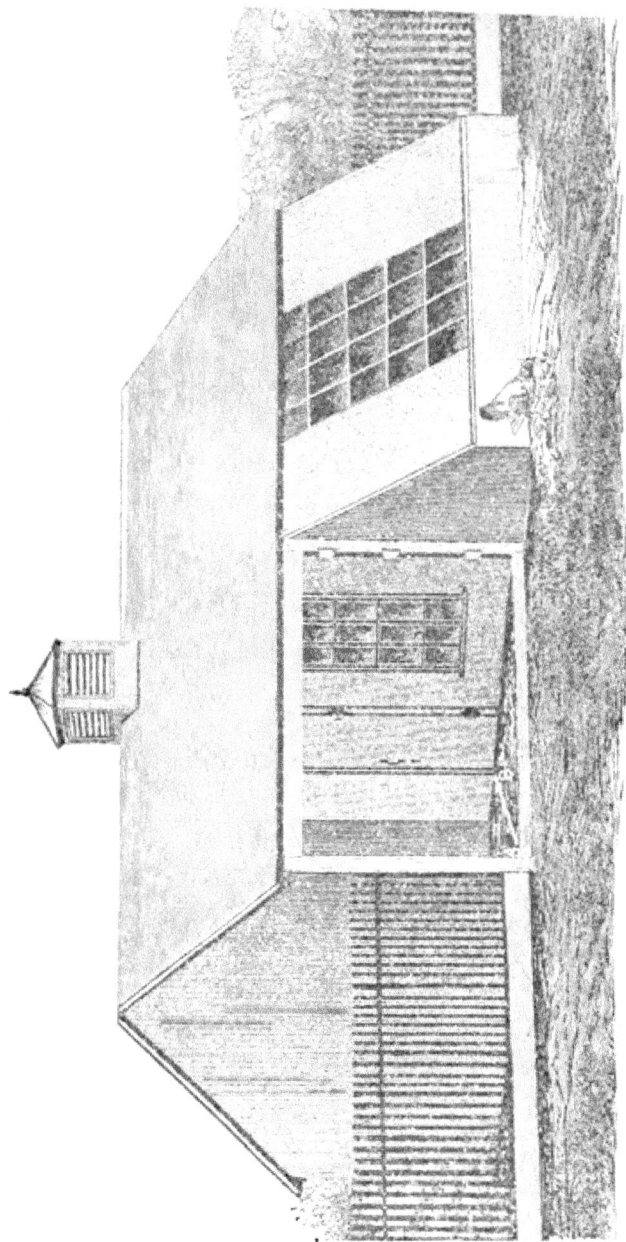

POULTRY HOUSE,

As used in day-time, with ten feet of front swung inside, to leave an open shed and form a partition dividing the roosting-room from the shed.

General Care of Poultry.

HOUSING.

We must, before cold weather puts in an appearance, make suitable quarters for our fowls. It will not do to let them "rough it" all day long about manure heaps or around dilapidated sheds when the snow is upon the ground if we want them to lay and come out in good condition for breeding the coming spring.

There is no need of putting up costly and elaborate buildings for fowls. It is very well for those who can afford it, and who like to have everything about their premises looking handsome and attractive; but for the novice who carries a slender purse, a plain and comfortable hennery will do as well.

The best site for a poultry house is an elevated one, but where that is not at hand, the ground should be ploughed or spaded, and the earth thrown towards the centre. When the frame is up, the floor should be raised to the top of the underpinning with gravelly loam and sand, and frequently renewed during the year.

The roosts should be low for Wyandottes or other large-sized breeds with a dropping board or trough under them. The nest boxes should be put in a quiet, secluded place, the dusting bin where the rays of the sun would fall upon it, and the ventilators should be placed in the roof.

In presenting this which we believe to be the most practical poultry house plan ever yet published, we, in explanation,

would impress upon all breeders the absolute importance of
air for our poultry to secure vitality in the egg. We may
house our stock closely through a long winter, and by high
feed and warm quarters secure their laying condition all
winter, even to that extent as to be quite marvelous.
Yet the eggs will not hatch. Their artificial and forced
mode of life and want of sulphur killing all vitality in the
life germ, and like a seed having no endosperm, have no
reproductive power. Fowls confined should be furnished
crushed charcoal and sulphur fed them in their soft feed at
least every five days, and greater still, the best of ventilation
secured for them. There is no place where they will select
to bask in the sun and dust themselves, in which they seem
to abandon themselves to recreation, as in an open shed
having a southern exposure. The house can be made double,
forty-four feet long, the two roosting rooms coming in the
center of the building, or made in a single tenement, like our
plan, twenty-two feet long, with a two-foot projection along
twelve feet of it, the remaining ten feet being a convertible
room, which can be used as an open shed, or the same may
be added to enlarge our room to twenty-two by fifteen feet
dimensions, which every fair day can be occupied from ten
A. M. to two P. M. as a shed in which the open air can be
enjoyed by the flock, no matter if the snow be ten feet deep;
and the swinging of this partition or front from A to B is a
far easier task than to shovel snow an hour that our pets
may enjoy the open air.

It will be seen that the small door is hinged to the swinging partition, and that it can be folded back before swinging
the partition to the front, thus it is the door by which you
enter your house in both cases. The five foot space from
edge of small door to rear of the house and across the
roosting room gives ample space for the platform over
which to erect the roosting poles for forty fowls, and
under which platform to arrange six or eight nests for

the flock. Our plan is: The rear posts five feet, front posts seven feet, the front roof eight and a half feet wide, rear roof eleven feet wide, the inclined plane of the projection is seven feet long, while the base of the same is twenty-two inches high, the projection being two feet at base. The cupola ventilator being three feet square, the same running down to within eight inches of the floor, with sliding traps in it near the roof to open in case of hot weather, the ventilation drawing from the bottom, thus taking the impure air from near the floor. The whole can be made of dressed spruce lumber, with not a stick in the frame larger than three by four for sills, with two by three scantling to nail the boards to; the whole to cost not over eighty-five dollars in single tenement, and one hundred and sixty dollars if built in a double tenement. This movable front, *i. e.*, partition, will add in expense the cost of hinges and trouble to make a substantial door of the same, over and above the stationary mode of structure.

HEALTH IN THE POULTRY YARD.

Every year we gain more knowledge of poultry breeding. Our own experience, coupled with that of others, gives us many new and interesting facts that aid us in our pursuit. Of late many scientists and intelligent fanciers have investigated the various causes which lead to sickness and mortality among fowls, and found that many of the ailments which afflict them can be traced to bad care, improper food and drink, and neglect of sanitary measures.

Domestic fowls are not exempt from the laws of nature, mortality and disease prey upon them as well as upon other living things. Yet, when we consider their countless numbers, their varied surroundings, and the causes which predispose them to sickness, we are surprised at their general good health, even under neglect and bad care.

We have always looked on the complex organism of the fowl with feelings of pleasure and admiration. One can see if they are properly cared for, they will enjoy better health than most any other domestic animal, owing to their active habits and varied food when at liberty.

When we see or hear of the ravages of disease sweeping off whole flocks in a neighborhood without malarial or atmospheric causes, while adjoining localities enjoy immunity from sickness, we are sure the sanitary laws were violated in one place and observed in the other. We cannot, however, face the broad fact and say our fowls won't die nor become diseased despite all the sanitary laws in existence. But what we wish to convey and impress is this, that a large percentage of our domestic poultry die or become diseased through neglect, carelessness and indifference of their keepers, that might be saved if they observed a few rules in their breeding, feeding, care and management.

It is false to assert that pure bred fowls are more liable to disease than birds promisciously bred. It is not in the purity nor the long continued selection of characteristic qualities and points, but in the way they are bred and raised. The breeder alone is to blame for most all the ailments and losses of the poultry yard, unknowingly and unsuspectingly, let us say in charity to him. And, while he may be studying and aiming to improve his fowls by his own method, he is, by the same false mode of reasoning, improving them off the face of the earth.

Our long experience with pure bred fowls of one or the other variety, and what we have gained through other reliable sources, only help to confirm us in all we have herein expressed. We are not alone in charging to breeders the ruinous effects of their misgovernment of the poultry yard, for the every day tale of sickness and death that we are permitted to hear while asking our advice, shows conclusively there is something radically wrong or "rotten in Denmark."

We do not believe much in doctoring sick fowls—far better the hatchet, for in most cases the sick bird is ailing several days, perhaps weeks before it is noticed, and the disease may have had time to seat itself, and though a cure may be effected for the time being, still it may leave the bird constitutionally weak and unfit to propagate a healthy offspring.

Breeders should endeavor to make a radical change in their way of breeding and raising thoroughbred poultry. We own it is hard to convince our people that their methods are wrong, but if they would for a moment think how important it is to breed from reliable, healthy stock, and how to secure health and thrift in the poultry yard, they would be convinced that they do too much pampering and coddling with young and old birds.

Veterans who have made their mark in the poultry business, can turn this leaf over. The suggestions are intended only for those who are remiss in their duties, and those who are trying to do too much. It is certain, however, we subject our fowls to too much artificial treatment, management and care from the hour they leave the shell. We are prone to pamper our exhibition birds and breeders with artificially prepared food, when it is a well known fact high living is antagonistic to fecundity.

How often do we hear of this and that breed being tender, that a large percentage of their eggs fail to hatch, and the few chicks which live to break the shell live long enough to behold a stronger race enjoying the bounties and beauties of nature, when the fact is, those breeds have been prominent with our ancestors, and esteemed for their vigor and fecundity.

Rather than to oppose those new breeds which are made up of good material, and bred uniformly for years to stamp them as new varieties, they should be hailed by every one who has the improvement of our domestic fowls at heart. There is no fear of the "old reliable" taking a back seat through all the periodic "booms," but will rather stimulate the breeders to greater improvement to keep them in the front rank to compete with the new breeds.

The struggle for mastery between the new breeds will evoke the zeal, skill and perseverance of Wyandotte breeders to maintain the popularity of their favorites. Already this new family has branched into several strains. Being a standard fowl, every breeder will do his level best to improve their qualities and make them creditable to the stock of the country.

Now, while you are going on improving and beautifying your Wyandottes, we will lay down a few rules for the guidance of beginners that may suggest something better or at least help a little in your breeding. First, be sure to purchase from reliable breeders; for, take our word for it, the country will soon be flooded with poor trash, many taking advantage of the growing popularity of the breed. Do not mate brother and sisters if you can avoid it, for incestuous breeding will sap the foundation of vigor and fecundity.

If you are in doubt about your fowls being healthy, the comb, gait and movements while walking, breathing when at rest, and the character of the droppings will generally give you a good idea of the state of their health.

A healthy fowl, in good condition of flesh, will have a rich, red comb, the comb much fuller in the laying season than when moulting, brooding or nursing the young. A fowl at rest will show the color of health in comb and face much better than when aroused or actively engaged, for then you can see the red coming and going alternately.

The fowl that does not sway its body with every step, its neck yielding to every motion, the head elevated and nodding with every movement of foot and body, you may be sure is ailing. A sick or ailing fowl will not sway its body when walking, but on the contrary, its body and neck will be drawn in, the head and tail carried low, the comb pale, evincing unusual thirst and a desire to be alone.

A fowl that shows a labored respiration, the body giving with each breath, a desire to doze, and while dozing recovers itself and shakes its head—that bird is ailing. The droppings of a sick fowl are usually in a semi-liquid state, and the color varies from dark brown to greenish. In cholera it assumes the color of sulphur mixed with green, the green being the last voided. In a healthy fowl the excrement is round and firm, of a dark gray color, showing light gray on top.

"An ounce of prevention is worth a pound of cure." This is so true of fowls that we might say it is worth a ton of cure and a year of labor. Feed your fowls regularly with varied food; keep fresh water always before them; clean their roosting places and runs often, and see that they are kept free from lice. In their drinking water put some tincture of iron or iron rust — old nails will answer the purpose — and a little of the Douglas Mixture between times.

We cannot, in a work like this, have much to say about diseases. We will mention a few of the most prevalent and dangerous, with the latest cures for the same.

Let us say your fowl is ailing from catarrh or roup: Inject a solution of carbolic acid into its nostrils, and wash out the mouth, face and eyes with the same or strong vinegar and alcohol. Feed warm mush with plenty of cayenne pepper, and make their drink strong of iodide of potassium. Dr. Monroe recommends sulphurous acid medication, by making the fowl inhale the fumes of sulphur sprinkled on some red-hot cinders.

Cholera has baffled the skill of the medical profession, therefore it would be presumptuous in us to say that this or that is a specific. However, lately several cases of genuine cholera have come under our observation. We saw a breeder in a fit of desperation make a strong decoction of tobacco leaves and mix it with meal, and those that could not eat were forced to swallow the mixture, and it cured every one. He has since then cured hogs of cholera by the same mixture.

VENTILATION.

Illy ventilated quarters, and the absence of sun and light, exert a powerful influence on the health of fowls. Without fresh air, sun and light, fowls would become like plants in a cellar—pale and sickly, unproductive and unprofitable. If every avenue by which the pure air of heaven can reach them is closed, they will stifle to death by fetid vapors, or else become victims of disease.

Ventilation is a safeguard and sanitary precaution against the ills arising from close confinement and overcrowded places. It is a matter of little trouble to ventilate the fowls' quarters in summer time. The removal of a window, door or board will serve for this purpose. But when winter, cold and cheerless, comes in, and the bleak winds blow through the leafless trees like a funeral dirge, we are put to our wits' end to know how to ventilate thoroughly without causing draughts to injure the fowls.

Heat is a condition of nature favorable for egg production and for putting on flesh. But if we make our henneries warm by artificial means or by massing a large number together, we are surely laying the foundation for their ruin. Artificial heat, however, is not as dangerous an enemy as the other, because it can be regulated at will and the temperature kept more evenly. But to flatter ourselves that the warmth of the fowls' bodies, coming in contact with one another, and the air which they breathe will be all-sufficient for their comfort and health, is a foolish and palpable error, as the sad, historical recollection of the Black Hole of Calcutta has proven.

Although warmth of body and the heat of the hen house may start the egg machinery going, only partial development of the egg functions are brought about; the conditions being unfavorable owing to the impurities arising from the droppings and exhalations of the fowls, and taken up again by the respiratory organs until the blood becomes poisoned and the system lowered to a degree to invite disease and death.

CONFINEMENT.

It is well known to those who are breeding Wyandottes, that these fowls will bear confinement better than the Asiatics, because they are more actively inclined. But we advise every breeder not to confine his birds if it can be avoided for no breed will do well in confinement.

Within the narrow limits of a fowl house there is not room for healthful exercise in warm weather. The birds will, in time, get out of condition and cease to lay. The ground becomes tainted and they feed on food defiled by their own excrement, which rapidly produces loss of health and condition. Cleanliness and good care will avert many of the consequent evils attending close confinement, but no kind of food will entirely compensate for the loss of pure air and agreeable exercise, so essential to good health.

In towns and cities one cannot always have the advantages of freedom so necessary to his fowls. In such cases the number should be reduced to conform to the size of their quarters and extent of their range. The runs should be frequently forked over except a small patch for grass. The turning under of the soil will deodorize the droppings and make the earth sweet and healthy.

Confinement without proper exercise will deteriorate the fowls and impair their organs of reproduction. Darwin says: "In Europe, close confinement has a marked effect on the fertility of the fowl; in France it has been found

that with fowls allowed considerable freedom twenty per
cent. only of their eggs fail to hatch, with less freedom
forty per cent. failed, and in close confinement sixty per
cent. were not hatched."

EXERCISE.

The more we study the habits of fowls, the more we are
impressed with the conviction that exercise is a necessity.
In confinement nothing is so conducive to the health and
productiveness of fowls as agreeable exercise. Food and
cleanliness will do much toward keeping them in thrift, but
if allowed to doze away upon the roosts or in the sunny
corner of the hennery day after day, without exercise of
some kind, they will soon learn vicious habits and become
useless as layers or breeders.

Idleness is the parent of mischief as well as of many ills
that afflict birds in close confinement. Under artificial ar-
rangements exercise can only be given by improvising ways
and means at our disposal. Scratching is a very agreeable
and natural way to give exercise, and to encourage the
fowls during the dreary days of winter and early spring,
scatter all the small grains among the loose earth of the
floor, leaves or chaff for them to scratch through and look
up the seeds or kernels. Burying the grains in sand or
coal ashes will also afford them pleasant employment.

It is not because the Wyandottes are good scratchers
that you should neglect to provide them with some loose
material when confined. We advise you to keep them busy
for much of their usefulness depends on their activity.
A lazy cock makes a poor stock getter, and a lazy lot of
hens make poor layers. Nor is it the large breeds alone
that depend on motion for thrift; the medium-sized and
the small breeds and all down to the diminutive Bantam require exercise to make them hardy, healthy and productive.

LICE AND PARASITES.

Vermin indirectly lead to sickness. These insidious pests, after they gain a foothold, harass the fowls day and night, keep them uneasy during roosting time when they should be at rest, and suck the juices and blood from their bodies irrespective of age or size. Lice multiply with great rapidity, the more filth the more vermin.

The cheapest and most effectual way of exterminating lice from fowls and the house is by rubbing through the fowls' feathers to the skin a mixture of carbolic acid and flour of sulphur when dry, and fumagation of the hen house with a liberal supply of whitewash put on hot. These materials are not expensive, are readily obtained and can be applied everywhere in the hennery. An ounce of carbolic acid to a pailful of whitewash will make it more effectual for killing these pests and their germs. In using the whitewash let us remind you not to spare the brush nor whitewash, but dash it into every crack and crevice and spread it over every spot in the hen house. The roosts and nest boxes should be well saturated with kerosene oil to destroy every vestige of these "festive pests," of course, avoiding the use of kerosene on sitting hens or in their nests.

In filthy hen houses one may look to the under parts of the perches and find that lice and parasites breed, brood and hive together in great numbers. This is horrible! But how complacently the careless breeder can look this "naked" fact in the face without wincing! He likes a nice fresh egg for breakfast and a tender broiler once in a while, but cannot see the necessity of keeping his fowls and fowl house clean.

THE DUST BATH.

The dust bath is to poultry Nature's cleanser and renovator and is as necessary for cleansing the feathers of fowls

from vermin and effete matter as a cool, pure water bath
is to the person of cleanly habits.   If we watch the habits
of all wild game birds, we can see them in the open clear-
ings and on the country roads at early sunrise dusting themselves as rapidly as possible.   And if we give our domestic
fowls a chance, we can see an instinctive desire in the
young as well as old to scratch, pulverize the earth and
adjust their feathers, and, by the rapid action of their claws,
dust themselves.   The bath is made more effective by
adding to it a pound of sulphur, mixing it thoroughly.

SELECTING EGGS FOR HATCHING.

A proper selection of eggs for setting is the first point
to be attended to in raising poultry.   The eggs should be
regular in shape, of good size, not the very largest, but the
most uniform, and from the best layers.   It requires some
experience to select the eggs from Wyandotte hens, because
some are more deeply tinged with " bloom " than others.

SETTING THE HENS.

Perhaps one of the most vexatious and annoying things
about poultry keeping is the hatching part.   It is physically,
and we presume to say morally, impossible to force or coax
a hen to sit if she don't want to.   Well, what are we to do
with our much-prized eggs?   If we cannot do better, it is
by far best to buy or borrow a sitting hen from our neigh-
bor.   In many cases one setting of eggs is worth more than
a dozen sitters of the common sort; and it is a plain matter
of economy to buy ordinary hens of farmers if you have no
broody hens yourself.

NESTS.

Now, supposing your " Dot " wants to sit,— what then?
Simply treat her as you would another hen.   Make a nice

clean nest for her, put in the bottom some earth or an
inverted sod, mould and fashion it in the same way as if she
made it herself put in a little cut straw on top, shake some
sulphur or tobacco dust over it, and place a few medicated
eggs in the nest, and move your sitter at nightfall quietly
and gently to the place prepared for her.

When your sitter draws the eggs under her, shuffles her
legs for the purpose of resting her breast upon them, ruffles
her feathers when you approach, and "cocks" one eye
sidewise to see if you mean to disturb her, there is every
reason to hope she means business and may be trusted with
valuable eggs.

It is well to remember, however, that during the time of
incubation the sitting hen should have food, water, gravel
and dust convenient. Corn is preferable, though a little
oats and barley occasionally are good. The dust bath is a
matter of necessity, for the broody fever generates lice, and
the sitter must rid herself of them or she may desert the
nest or ruin the chicks.

THE CARE OF CHICKS.

It is an easy matter, ordinarily, to get the chicks hatched
out if the sitter faithfully performs her duty, and the eggs are
fresh and fertile when put under her. But to care for them
afterward, and bring them safely through the early stage of
growth from the time they leave the shell till they can be
trusted to an open coop outside of doors is a more difficult
task, much care is necessary to prevent mortality among
them in our cold and changeable climate.

The early broods should be kept in a barn or close shed
where there is no danger from cats, rats or other poultry
enemies till they become strong. If the weather be cold
and wet, keep them in awhile longer, and then they may be
put out in a sunny spot with the hen in a coop.

April, though considered a good month for hatching chicks, is sometimes very fickle. Often we have plenty of sunshine and showers, and again Winter lingers in the lap of Spring. However, it is best to be prepared for the worst, and provide for the young chicks a close coop with a light of glass neatly fitted in one side to admit the warmth of the sun, and a sliding bottom well covered with dry earth and sand until the weather becomes genial and the ground dry and warm.

Chicks do not require any food the first day they break the shell. Bread crumbs and hard boiled eggs, with milk to drink, make the most suitable and agreeable diet to begin with. A week of such feeding, with a little boiled meat occasionally, will help them along nicely if they be kept warm during the days and nights. "Variety is the spice of life" for either young or old birds, and a gradual change to heartier food will be relished by the growing chicks.

The traditional corn meal dough must be avoided in the beginning—in fact it can be dispensed with entirely. Broken rice, cracked wheat, millet seed, oatmeal, johnnycake and brown bread constitute a wholesome and nutritious diet. But if the chicks cannot procure insects, bits of boiled liver and cut onions may be given with the best results. Feed often and a little at a time until they feather out. The last meal at night should be wheat, barley or cracked corn.

POULTRY INTERESTS.

We should consider this volume incomplete if we did not say something about the progress and improvement of domestic poultry in our own times. It is really pleasant to recall to mind what has been done in the past three decades toward the prosperity of the poultry interests of America. Few persons could predict the vast progress, improvement and product of this industry in stock, in building and in capital invested in one way or another within the short span of one generation.

Heretofore the poultry business was looked upon as a small thing, only adapted to cripples and superannuated people. He is only a "chicken man," was formerly a remark not infrequently heard from some ignoramus, into whose narrow heart the love of the beautiful in nature never penetrated. How is it now, dear reader? The value and importance of the poultry industry as a source of wealth to the country is far beyond the ideas of those who have given it a mere passing thought, or given it any attention at all.

Few of the early pioneers are now living to see the fruits of their first labors and perseverance. Well done ! we can say of their work. This cannot now be denied even by those who years ago opposed the fancier's efforts at improvement in the different breeds of fowls, believing that it was a grand scheme, born of poultry fanciers, simply for the purpose of selling fowls at high prices and of no special value to the farmer or housekeeper.

Improvement in domestic poultry is of slow growth, though under the guardianship of the human race for thousands of years. But, with the dawn of progress, characteristic qualities were established which separated forever the thoroughbred from the common stock, and the value of the improved breeds rose steadily as their usefulness became known.

Men of means, intelligence and taste care nothing about common stock of any kind, There is nothing about it that is valuable or interesting to study as compared to thoroughbred fowls which have been bred to a degree of uniformity, beauty, utility and excellence. Already some of the best men in the country are engaged in the laudable work of cultivating and improving our poultry stock. Every month since the original excitement of the "chicken business," the number has increased till we can count them by thousands scattered over the broad domain of the United States. And still they come!

The sound and practical knowledge wielded by the poultry press generally is a powerful lever in the fulcrum of our industry, while those engaged in keeping poultry generously support their favorite papers, and in return re. ceive the greatest aid from the many hints, suggestions and thorough information of every detail connected with the cultivation of improved fowls. And yet what is most desired now is that our poultry publications—while keeping up with every improvement and advocating the skillful culture properly attained in the constant improvement of poultry by the special breeders of birds for exhibition, having the highest points of excellence in symmetry, plumage and weight—should not fail to publish the experiments made in the direction of utility by all interested in this specialty.

The profits accruing from the cultivation of poultry, where it is conducted in an economical and judicious way, amount to a snug sum annually. The keeping of poultry as a business or secondary pursuit has become a means of money getting; and while it adds pleasure and recreation as an employment, it is a branch of home industry that has fully as much cash value at its command as any other industrial branch in the country.

To make the keeping of poultry profitable, it is necessary that ways and means should first be provided. No domestic animal will thrive and be productive if it is kept in a half-starved and neglected condition ; and it is folly to expect fowls to lay and put on flesh when they have not the material at hand to do it with. To be profitable it is also necessary that the better kinds be kept; that suitable places be provided for their accommodation, and that they be properly fed and carefully and intelligently managed.

There is no question of doubt but the keeping of poultry is a profitable source of income. Little springs unite to swell mighty rivers. The demand for prime fowls is increasing annually, and the prices are much steadier than in years past, while the greatest profits are derived from the successful manner of keeping and managing the stock. Poultry can be converted into money while living or dead, and one has not to wait for years before he gets some of the benefits from his labor, outlay and care, as they are a product always marketable, whether in the form of eggs or flesh.

It is certain fowls have been greatly undervalued in past years as a means of recreation, but now-a-days the breeding of improved stock has become one of the most important and remunerative pursuits in this country.

To-day there are few industries in the United States that show a healthier growth or yield so fast a return to the American people in comparison to the amount of capital required and employed in carrying it on. But, after all, it appears strange to us why our enterprising countrymen, who have a national aptitude for every pursuit there is money in, can look at the poultry business with its vast channels of supply and demand, its rapid growth and influence, its social and pecuniary importance, and not more generally engage in the cultivation of poultry as a source of profit and amusement.

It is absurd to suppose that thousands of our best business men—bankers, lawyers, doctors, ministers and mechanics would engage in the pursuit and follow it up for years as an occupation if it did not pay, and afford at the same time an agreeable pastime. One thing which favors it a great deal is the division of labor. The man of limited means, though commencing on a small scale, has the same chance to breed, sell and exhibit as the man of capital, for there cannot be any monoply in the poultry business.

It is impossible to give a correct statement of the value of the poultry industry of the United States. Often it has been said that the value of the business as a source of wealth to the country has not been fully estimated; its magnitude is far beyond the ideas of those even who have given some thought and attention to the subject.

From reliable statistics at hand we find the number of eggs produced in the whole United States in 1880 to be upward of 9,000,000,000, valued at $240,000,000. The value of poultry consumed in the United States for the same year was estimated at $300,000,000. The total of the two items is $540,000,000, representing the value of the poultry and eggs consumed by the people of the United States.

But these figures do not include the amount of fancy poultry and eggs sold for breeding stock, nor of the stock kept for breeding purposes, which makes quite an item of itself and is increasing yearly.

There is a wide field for American fanciers to work in. The great West with its millions of acres yet untouched, and the sunny South, just awakening to its own interests, will have to be supplied, and all will join hands and carry the industry to the golden shores of the Pacific, and establish a permanent and paying business for every one who knowingly and attentively cultivates thoroughbred poultry.